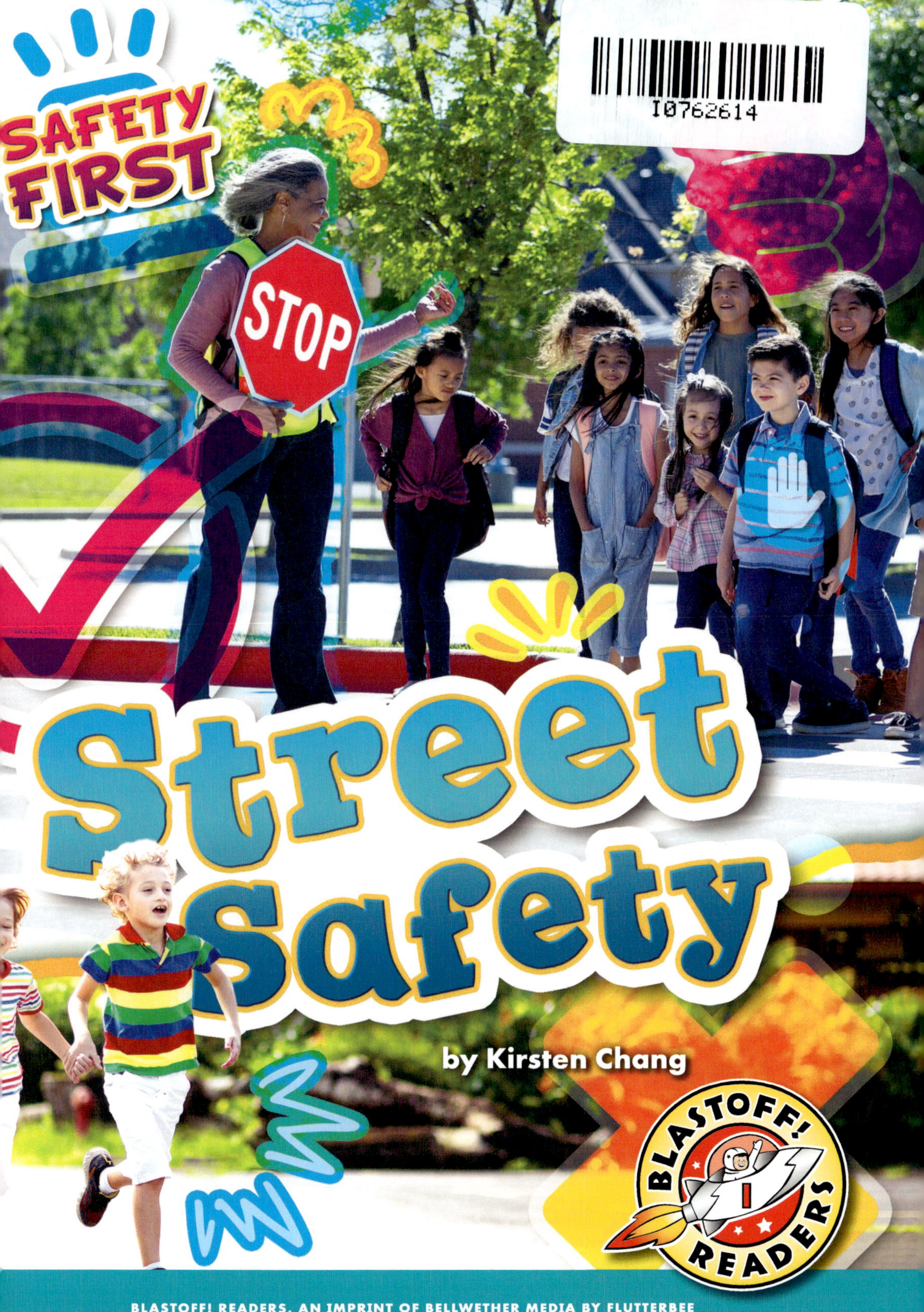

Street Safety

by Kirsten Chang

BLASTOFF! READERS, AN IMPRINT OF BELLWETHER MEDIA BY FLUTTERBEE

Blastoff! Readers are carefully developed by literacy experts to build reading stamina and move students toward fluency by combining standards-based content with developmentally appropriate text.

Level 1 provides the most support through repetition of high-frequency words, light text, predictable sentence patterns, and strong visual support.

Level 2 offers early readers a bit more challenge through varied sentences, increased text load, and text-supportive special features.

Level 3 advances early-fluent readers toward fluency through increased text load, less reliance on photos, advancing concepts, longer sentences, and more complex special features.

★ **Blastoff! Universe**

Reading Level

Grade K

Grades 1–3

Grade 4

This edition first published in 2027 by Bellwether Media, Inc.

For information regarding permission, write to Bellwether Media, Inc., Attention: Permissions Department, 3500 American Blvd W, Suite 150, Bloomington, MN 55431.

Library of Congress Cataloging-in-Publication Data is available at www.loc.gov or upon request from the publisher.

ISBN: 9798898800383 (hardcover)
ISBN: 9798898802912 (paperback)
ISBN: 9798898801625 (ebook)

Editor: Rachael Barnes Designer: Andrea Schneider

Printed in the United States of America, North Mankato, MN.

Table of Contents

Safe on the Street

Walt uses the **crosswalk**. He makes it across the street safely!

crosswalk

Why Stay Safe?

Young kids should not cross the street on their own. They could get hurt.

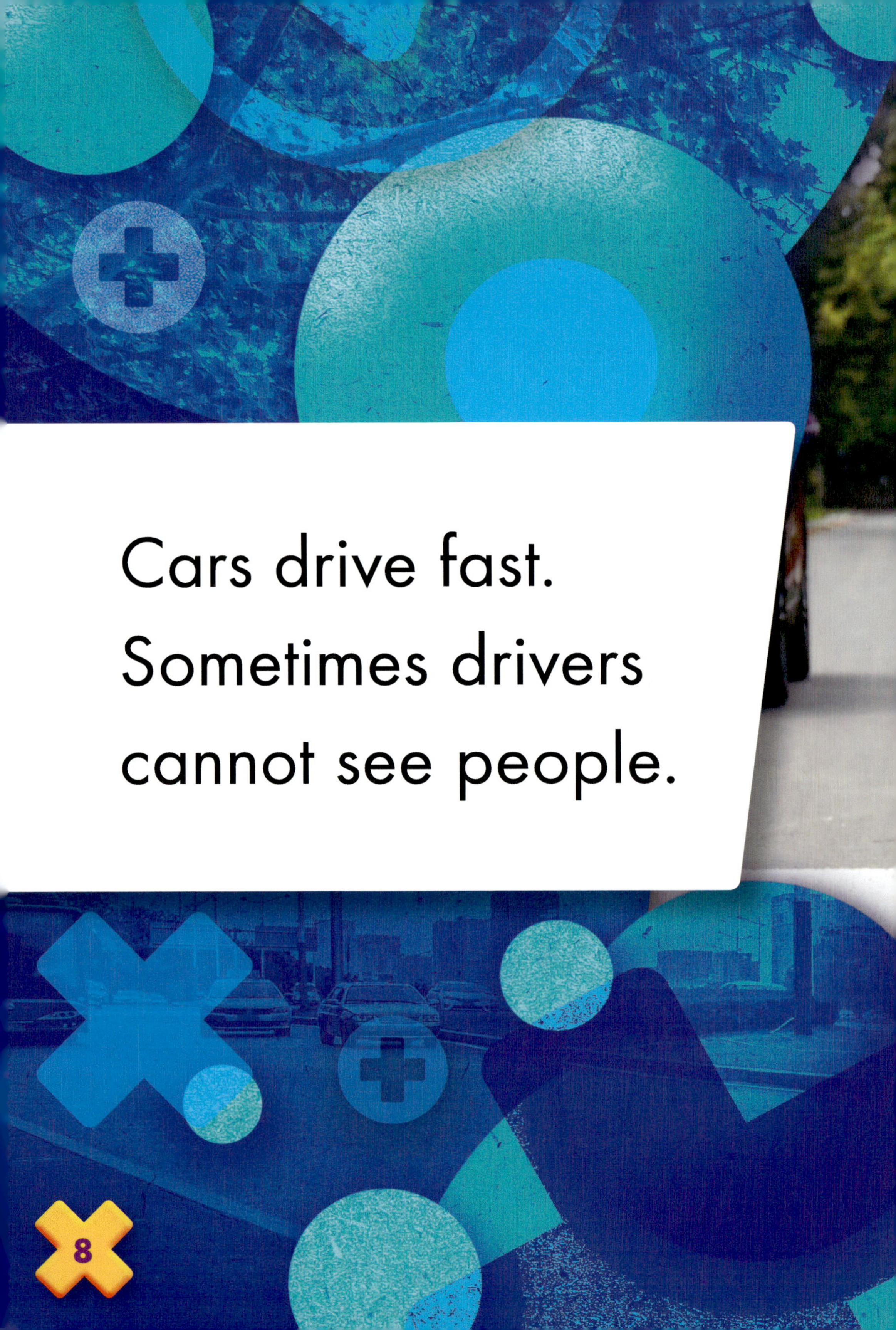

Cars drive fast. Sometimes drivers cannot see people.

30

We are careful at night. People can be hard to see in the dark!

Staying Safe

Kai's ball rolls away! He does not chase it. He asks Mom for help.

Mina walks on the sidewalk. A car starts backing out of a driveway. She stops.

Felix and Mom stop at the curb. They look both ways for **traffic**.

How to Cross the Street

- Young kids **wait** for an adult.
- **Stop** at the curb.
- **Look** left, right, then left again.
- **Keep looking** for traffic until safely across.

These friends wait at the crosswalk. The walk **signal** changes. Time to cross!

walk signal

Look! There is a **crossing guard**. We follow her **directions** to stay safe.

Safety Rules
STOP
Never run into the street.
Walk on the sidewalk.
Look carefully for traffic.
Cross only at street corners or crosswalks.
STOP
crossing guard

Glossary

crossing guard

a person whose job is to help people cross busy streets

crosswalk

a specially marked place to cross a street

directions

instructions about what to do

signal

a sign at a crosswalk that tells people when to walk

traffic

the movement of people and vehicles along a street

To Learn More

AT THE LIBRARY

Catena, Melissa. *Road Safety*. Minneapolis, Minn.: Jump!, 2025.

Chang, Kirsten. *Bike Safety*. Minneapolis, Minn.: Bellwether Media, 2027.

Korté, Steve. *Look Both Ways, Scooby-Doo!: A Guide to Road Safety*. North Mankato, Minn.: Capstone, 2025.

ON THE WEB

FACTSURFER

Factsurfer.com gives you a safe, fun way to find more information.

1. Go to www.factsurfer.com.
2. Enter "street safety" into the search box and click 🔍.
3. Select your book cover to see a list of related content.

Index

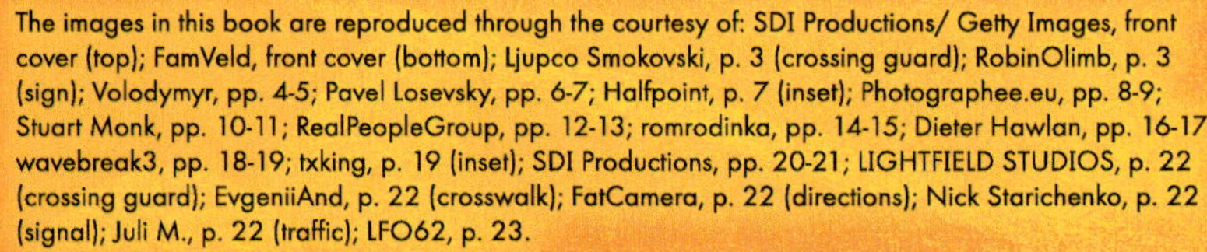

The images in this book are reproduced through the courtesy of: SDI Productions/ Getty Images, front cover (top); FamVeld, front cover (bottom); Ljupco Smokovski, p. 3 (crossing guard); RobinOlimb, p. 3 (sign); Volodymyr, pp. 4-5; Pavel Losevsky, pp. 6-7; Halfpoint, p. 7 (inset); Photographee.eu, pp. 8-9; Stuart Monk, pp. 10-11; RealPeopleGroup, pp. 12-13; romrodinka, pp. 14-15; Dieter Hawlan, pp. 16-17; wavebreak3, pp. 18-19; txking, p. 19 (inset); SDI Productions, pp. 20-21; LIGHTFIELD STUDIOS, p. 22 (crossing guard); EvgeniiAnd, p. 22 (crosswalk); FatCamera, p. 22 (directions); Nick Starichenko, p. 22 (signal); Juli M., p. 22 (traffic); LFO62, p. 23.